GLOBAL ISSUES B

Series editors: Stephen Hayn

*E*CONOMIC
*J*USTICE

Jana L. Webb

6 Studies
for individuals
or groups

INTERVARSITY PRESS
DOWNERS GROVE, ILLINOIS 60515

InterVarsity Press is the book-publishing division of InterVarsity Christian Fellowship, a student movement active on campus at hundreds of universities, colleges and schools of nursing in the United States of America, and a member movement of the International Fellowship of Evangelical Students. For information about local and regional activities, write Public Relations Dept., InterVarsity Christian Fellowship, 6400 Schroeder Rd., P.O. Box 7895, Madison, WI 53707-7895.

All Scripture quotations, unless otherwise indicated, are from the Holy Bible, New International Version. Copyright © 1973, 1978, International Bible Society. Used by permission of Zondervan Bible Publishers.

Cover illustration: TransLight

ISBN 0-8308-4906-8

Printed in the United States of America

12	11	10	9	8	7	6	5	4	3	2	1
99	98	97	96	95	94	93	92	91	90		

Contents

Because humankind is made in the image of God, every person, regardless of race, religion, color, culture, class, sex or age, has an intrinsic dignity because of which he or she should be respected and served, not exploited. Here too we express penitence both for our neglect and for having sometimes regarded evangelism and social concern as mutually exclusive.

Although reconciliation with people is not reconciliation with God, nor is social action evangelism, nor is political liberation salvation, nevertheless we affirm that evangelism and sociopolitical involvement are both part of our Christian duty. For both are necessary expressions of our doctrines of God and humankind, our love for our neighbor and our obedience to Jesus Christ.

The message of salvation implies also a message of judgment upon every form of alienation, oppression and discrimination, and we should not be afraid to denounce evil and injustice wherever they exist.

—*Lausanne Covenant, Article Five.*

Welcome to Global Issues Bible Studies

With all the rapid and dramatic changes happening in our world today, it's easy to be overwhelmed and simply withdraw. But it need not be so for Christians! God has not only given us the mandate to love the world, he has given us the Holy Spirit and the community of fellowship to guide us and equip us in the ministry of love.

Ministering in the world can be threatening: It requires change in both our lifestyle and our thinking. We end up discovering that we need to cling closer to Jesus than ever before—and that becomes the great personal benefit of change. God's love for the world is the same deep love he has for you and me.

This study series is designed to help us understand what is going on in *the world*. Then it takes us to *the Word* to help us be faithful in our compassionate response. The series is firmly rooted in the evangelical tradition which calls for a personal saving relationship with Jesus Christ and a public lifestyle of discipleship that demonstrates the Word has truly come alive in us.

At the front of the guide is an excerpt from the Lausanne Covenant which we have found particularly helpful. We have developed this series in keeping with the spirit of the covenant, especially sections four and five. You may wish to refer to the Lausanne Covenant for further guidance as you form your own theology of evangelism and social concern.

In the words of the covenant's authors we place this challenge before you: "The salvation we claim should be transforming us in the totality of our personal and social responsibilities. Faith without works is dead."

Getting the Most from Global Issues Bible Studies
Global Issues Bible Studies are designed to be an exciting and challenging way to help us seek God's will for all of the world as it is found in Scripture. As we learn more about the world, we will learn more about ourselves as well.

How They Are Designed
Global Issues Bible Studies have a number of distinctive features. First, each guide has an introduction from the author which will help orient us to the subject at hand and the significant questions which the studies will deal with.

Second, the Bible study portion is inductive rather than deductive. In other words, the author will lead us to discover what the Bible says about a particular topic through a series of questions rather than simply telling us what he or she believes. Therefore, the studies are thought-provoking. They help us to think about the meaning of the passage so that we can truly understand what the biblical writer intended to say.

Third, the studies are personal. Global Issues Bible Studies are not just theoretical studies to be considered in private or discussed in a group. These studies will motivate us to action. They will expose us to the promises, assurances, exhortations and challenges of God's

Word. Through the study of Scripture, we will renew our minds so that we can be transformed by the Spirit of God.

Fourth, the guides include resource sections that will help you to act on the challenges Scripture has presented you with.

Fifth, these studies are versatile. They are designed for student, mission, neighborhood and/or church groups. They are also effective for individual study.

How They Are Put Together

Global Issues Bible Studies also have a distinctive format. Each study need take no more than forty-five minutes in a group setting or thirty minutes in personal study—unless you choose to take more time.

Each guide has six studies. If the guides are used in pairs, they can be used within a quarter system in a church and fit well in a semester or trimester system on a college campus.

The guides have a workbook format with space for writing responses to each question. This is ideal for personal study and allows group members to prepare in advance for the discussion. In addition the last question in each study offers suggestions and opportunity for personal response.

At the end of the guides are some notes for leaders. They describe how to lead a group discussion, give helpful tips on group dynamics and suggest ways to deal with problems which may arise during the discussion. With such helps, someone with little or no experience can lead an effective study.

Suggestions for Individual Study

1. As you begin the study, pray that God will help you understand and apply the passages to your life. Pray that he will show you what kinds of action he would have you take as a result of your time of study.

2. In your first session take time to read the introduction to the entire guide. This will orient you to the subject at hand and the author's goals for the studies.

3. Read the short introduction to the study.

4. Read and reread the suggested Bible passages to familiarize yourself with them.

5. A good modern translation of the Bible, rather than the King James Version or a paraphrase, will give you the most help. The New International Version, the New American Standard Bible and the Revised Standard Version are all recommended. The questions in this guide are based on the New International Version.

6. Use the space provided to respond to the questions. This will help you express your understanding of the passage clearly.

7. Look up the passages listed under *For Further Study* at the end of each study. This will help you to better understand the principles outlined in the main passages and give you an idea of how these themes are found throughout Scripture.

8. It might be good to have a Bible dictionary handy. Use it to look up any unfamiliar words, names or places.

9. Take time with the final question in each study to commit yourself to action and/or a change in attitude.

Suggestions for Group Study

1. Come to the study prepared. Follow the suggestions for individual study mentioned above. You will find that careful preparation will greatly enrich your time spent in group discussion.

2. Be willing to participate in the discussion. The leader of your group will not be lecturing. Instead, he or she will be encouraging the members of the group to discuss what they have learned. The leader will be asking the questions that are found in this guide.

3. Stick to the topic being discussed. Your answers should be based on the verses which are the focus of the discussion and not on outside authorities such as commentaries or speakers.

4. Be sensitive to the other members of the group. Listen attentively when they describe what they have learned. You may be surprised by their insights! When possible, link what you say to the comments of others. Also, be affirming whenever you can. This will encourage

some of the more hesitant members of the group to participate.

5. Be careful not to dominate the discussion. We are sometimes so eager to express our thoughts that we leave too little opportunity for others to respond. By all means participate! But allow others to also.

6. Expect God to teach you through the passage being discussed and through the other members of the group. Pray that you will have an enjoyable and profitable time together, but also that as a result of the study, you will find ways that you can take action individually and/or as a group.

7. If you are the discussion leader, you will find additional suggestions at the back of the guide.

God bless you in your adventure of love.

Steve Hayner
Gordon Aeschliman

Introducing Economic Justice

During recess, the White policemen drove their vehicles onto the playground of a junior high school in Soweto and opened fire on children innocently at play. Over their megaphones, the police announced that these kids had not seen anything yet—if they figured they could overthrow the apartheid system. As dozens of children lay dying on the ground, the police turned and drove away.

A prominent evangelical pastor of a Soweto church had to minister to grieving parents who lost children to this carnage. Seventeen kids from his church were among the dead. "Why does God hate us?" was the cry of these parents during the funeral. "Where is the justice?"

The pastor opened the Scriptures to them and talked of God's anger at the oppressor:

Can a corrupt throne be allied with you—

one that brings on misery by its decrees?
They band together against the righteous
    and condemn the innocent to death.
But the LORD has become my fortress,
    and my God the rock in whom I take refuge.
He will repay them for their sins
    and destroy them for their wickedness;
the LORD our God will destroy them. (Ps 94:20-23)

Woe to those who make unjust laws,
    to those who issue oppressive decrees,
to deprive the poor of their rights
    and withhold justice from the oppressed of my people,
making widows their prey
    and robbing the fatherless.
What will you do on the day of reckoning,
    when disaster comes from afar?
To whom will you run for help?
    Where will you leave your riches?
Nothing will remain but to cringe among the captives
    or fall among the slain.
Yet for all this, [God's] anger is not turned away,
    his hand is still upraised. (Is 10:1-4)

Not only do Blacks in South Africa suffer under a legalized system of oppression, but they suffer under a system that is practically run by the White church.

South Africa has a higher percentage of churchgoers within its population than any other country in the world. More than seventy per cent of its Whites are in church every Sunday. In this small nation of thirty million, more than fifty per cent of the world's gold and seventy per cent of the world's diamonds are mined. Yet, fifty per cent of Blacks are unemployed. Two hundred thousand Black children die of starvation every year, and only one doctor exists for every nineteen thousand Black residents.

The injustices of South Africa derive from the systematic decisions of the Whites to extract cheap labor from a Black slave-labor pool for great economic gain. And the outcome is absolutely devastating for the Black population. Justice could easily come to South Africa. All it would take is a spiritual revival among Whites who take seriously Christ's command to "love your neighbor as yourself."

The issues are similar in other countries. For instance, in the United States the church has yet to take leadership in rectifying the evils: the near-annihilation of Native Americans, the destruction of the Black family through slavery, the unfair land deals with Mexico, and the oppressive labor practices with Latino aliens.

Justice is not a liberal agenda. It's the character of God expressed in a society in which people decide to live in peace and true love. The church has been given the privilege of being at the forefront of this calling in the world today, bringing hope to the downtrodden that God can really meet them at their point of anguish. This is just the sort of good news those Soweto mothers wait to experience.

Because we live in a world where the welfare of distant nations and their inhabitants is so intertwined, justice is an international issue. Christians who love God must have a sincere desire to understand issues of justice.

Global Economy

Ours is a global economy—no matter how one views it. Inhabitants of this planet are inseparably linked through economic structures that have the potential to benefit many, but in reality bring prosperity to only a select few. From interest rates and oil prices to trade tariffs and foreign debt, the world's economy makes us truly interdependent. The North depends on the South for raw materials and inexpensive labor. The South, in turn, depends on the North for food consumed by its masses and capital to revitalize its stagnant economies.

The reality of this interdependence can be illustrated in the production of a garment. Although it bears the name of one country on its label (for example, "Made in the Philippines"), one can be certain that the thread, buttons, dye, material, scissors, pattern and sewing machine were manufactured in various countries and imported to the country where the garment is sewn. Ironically, the finished product will be shipped to and sold in another country (usually one in the North), even though the country that manufactured it has a greater need for it.

Unfortunately, our global economy is suffering from a severe case of partiality. Kingdom principles such as justice and righteousness are not evident. While the twenty-five Northern industrialized countries are boasting about their combined Gross National Product (GNP)—now an astronomical $8.2 trillion—the developing nations of the South must subsist on less than one-sixth of this wealth.

For example, countries in sub-Saharan Africa are among the poorest countries in the world. In 1988, their GNP per capita was only about $280. That is less than one-fifth of the per capita GNP of the middle-income countries of Latin America and Asia, and a mere four per cent of the average wage in North America.

Compounding the problem is the debt crisis. In 1988 nearly $100 billion (of which approximately fifty per cent was interest) was transferred from poor countries to rich countries to service the debt burden of the former. During the same year, it is estimated, developing countries lost nearly $100 due to severely biased trade policies. On top of this, there is substantial capital flight—that is, large amounts of capital flowing from the South to the North to purchase property, invest in stocks or store up large amounts of capital in private banks. Surely God is not endorsing these inequities and injustices, for he says that he loves, delights in and executes justice.

Another yardstick of global economic inequities is the policies of the international financial community—all of which favor the financially (and politically) powerful industrialized nations. This is vividly illustrated by transnational corporations. They now have a staggering annual turnover of more than $3.1 trillion—equivalent to almost thirty per cent of the gross world product. Total Third World debt (estimated to be one trillion dollars) thus amounts to a mere one-third of the yearly sales of these top two hundred firms, or about ten per cent of the world's yearly economic activity (now estimated at about ten trillion dollars).

Poverty, like a curtain, has descended to the earth, separating its citizens into two worlds. Population estimates of the Northern minority report that not more than twenty per cent of the world's inhabitants consume roughly seventy per cent of the world's goods and services, over fifty per cent of its agricultural products, and sixty per cent of its energy and other natural resources. The result of these inequities is poverty—appalling poverty.

But what does poverty really mean for the vast majority of the men, women and children in the world for whom Christ died? Statistically, it means that more than one billion people (more than the populations of North America, Europe, Japan and Australia combined) subsist on less than $200 per year. And "subsist" is clearly an understatement. Nine hundred million people are malnourished, and about half of these are starving—waiting to die any day. In 1990 it was estimated that seventy million voiceless people would die that year of starvation.

An advertisement in *Time* magazine during the late 1970s portrayed three children fighting for a meager plate of food. The caption read, "Some kids just never grow up—they die of hunger." For these children, death will be slow and agonizing—and made even more tragic by the fact that more than seventy million Americans are significantly overweight.

Poverty brings terrible diseases. Every day, nearly 35,000 children in the Third World between infancy and age five die from a preventable disease. In just three days, more children die than all the people who died during the Vietnam War. It is estimated that three million of these children die annually from diarrhea and other gastrointestinal diseases caused by the lack of clean water. Meanwhile, another 1.5 million die from measles or malaria because their countries cannot afford the vaccines and other medications.

Poverty also means hard labor for low wages. The parents of these malnourished and diseased children labor from dawn to dusk for mere handfuls of rice or a few small yams. Women are a rapidly growing segment of the wage (sweat)-labor force. In most countries, they work the same number of hours and days as men, but they are often less nourished, and many carry unborn children in their wombs. A staggering 850 million are illiterate. Many are indebted to their employers or landlords. Overworked, underfed, ignorant, diseased, harassed, helpless and hopeless, they have no knowledge of the gospel or the fact that they were made in the image of God.

Countries are inflicting untold pain and death upon their populations in order to invest in banks and property in the North, to buy luxury items for tourists and the elite citizens, and to pay mounting foreign debt.

Winners, Losers and Those Who Barely Play the Game

The tragedy of the debt crisis is not that Third World governments find it almost impossible to service their debt, but that most often it is the poor in each country who are called upon to repay loans for which they are not responsible and from which they in most cases have not benefited.

A case in point is Zambia, a low-income country in sub-Saharan Africa. Its $5 billion debt has become an impossible burden since the price of copper collapsed. Since the debt crisis, many who were once regarded as middle class according to Zambian standards have fallen into a new stratum—the *nouveau pauvre,* or new poor. Families that at one time were well-off economically are today barely surviving.

Many foods, medicines and other goods are no longer imported into the country because of the International Monetary Fund's (IMF) austerity program, which was instituted in 1986. (The IMF is part messenger, part watchdog for the industrialized countries that hold great economic power.) The result is uncontrollable inflation, which touched off a riot among thousands of urban poor in the streets of Lusaka, the capital. After some time and much damage, the government reinstituted food subsidies, but medicines and other goods are still very scarce.

The residents of Lusaka are most definitely losers in our global economy. They illustrate the influence of the forces of darkness in our world systems. Unfortunately, they are not alone. There are at least fifty other countries in Africa and Latin America that are in the same predicament. This cluster of nations, known as the low-income least-developed countries (LDCs), cannot service their debt on their current schedules. They are therefore placed on a blacklist by the IMF and told that they are not creditworthy, since servicing their huge debts has become a problem.

What of their malnourished, disease-ridden, overworked poor? Their need, according to the IMF's managing director, is the fault of their own government for failing to allocate its funding properly. How the funds are distributed among various social groups and among various public-expenditure categories (arms spending or social projects, productive investment or current operation) is a question decided by governments, he says. An international institution such as the IMF cannot take upon itself the role of dictating social and political objectives to sovereign governments.

This argument is half-baked—to put it politely.

The IMF has enormous influence on the economic and political choices of its heavily indebted clients. If it chose to do so, it could have tremendous impact because of the simple fact that, in this corrupt economic system, money talks. If the IMF's directors believed that economic growth can also result from greater social equality and access to education, health care, and other basic services, they could quite readily make such objectives part of the IMF's agenda. Unfortunately, they have not chosen to do so.

Shouldn't economic justice be the criterion by which one's treatment of the most vulnerable members of society is judged? For kingdom people, economic justice must be the standard we hold up in the midst of a biased economic system. We must be the voice of justice in an age of darkness.

Another group of Third World countries are commonly known as the middle-income LDCs. Most of these are in Latin America and Asia. This group has a combined debt of $650 billion (two-thirds of the total foreign debt owed by all countries), sixty-five per cent of which is owed to commercial banks. At the end of 1988, Brazil owed no less than $120 billion and Mexico $100 billion. Yet these countries are rich in natural resources and have a somewhat developed and diversified industrial structure. The IMF and commercial banks have allowed these countries to reschedule their debts, spreading out the short-term loan payments over several years. Given enough time, the right policies, and a decrease in interest rates, inflation and capital flight, it appears that these countries will be able to stabilize their economies and reduce their debt burdens by their own actions.

Despite this encouraging bit of news, these countries are far from winners. They are those who barely play the game, struggling from one fiscal year to the next, sweating blood so that they will not miss a payment on their debt. Despite their efforts, there have not been marked improvements in the balance sheets of the commercial banks and international agencies. It seems as though there is a lot of paper being shuffled around—but not much of it is currency.

The middle-income countries are like a ship in the middle of a tempest, a ship whose captain has noticed that his vessel has sprung a slow leak. The low-income countries, on the other hand, are like a small boat in the same tempest, full of passengers who are bailing out the water entering through a huge gouge in their vessel, while sharks circle the boat.

How can Zambia, Brazil or any other Third World country recover while the pressure is so intense? And why should the government or the poor within these countries be blamed for the vacillations in the world economy over which they have no control?

Surely the leaders of industrialized countries and international lending institutions know that they are in the driver's seat. Decisions they make about the economy deeply affect the low- and middle-income countries. Even the growth and stability that lead to economic recovery are determined by external conditions in the North, such as trade policies (protectionism, high tariffs and low prices for commodities), interest rates, inflation, capital flight, and national and international structures that maintain the solvency of Northern banks and protect them from the consequences of their poor lending decisions.

Do you suppose that directors of the IMF and its banks ever considered the environment that they have created within the global economy?

In most cases it would seem that the only well-being the IMF considered was that of the commercial banks, and all the commercial banks considered was their bottom-line profit.

Fighting Back

Poorer nations have banded together in hopes of leveraging their political and economic weight. In 1974 they created the New International Economic Order (NIEO), not only proposing but indeed demanding improvements in terms of trade, higher prices for Third World commodities, sharing of technology, and easier credit terms for external debt. Ignoring these demands, they say, would severely damage trade relationships and destabilize the world economy. The United Nations Conference on Trade and Development (UNCTAD), which took place in June 1979 in Manila, is another joint effort whose aim was to re-establish and promote additional North-South and South-South trade and development.

Critics of the NIEO and UNCTAD have been quick to point out flaws—some go so far as to predict failure. Of course, the more ideological advocates of free enterprise say that free trade and a political climate conducive to business investment will of themselves provide the key to overcoming the poverty and debt burden of the Third World. One critic believes that the call for a new international economic order by the leaders of the Third World is a sham, a fraud designed to divert the attention of these countries' people from the internal structures that block development and keep the people poor. Some of this criticism may have merit. Justice in Zambia and Brazil does not necessarily mean justice for all Zambians or Brazilians. It may mean justice for only the elites of those countries.

Response from God's Kingdom People

In many parts of the world today evangelical Christians can take very little positive action to effect change at national and international levels. This is often attributed to the small size of the Christian community, the lack of international support, and—most often—the absence of legislation to protect human rights. These believers trust God to move evil systems and structures that threaten not only their scarce freedoms but also their very lives.

Many of us, however, live, work and worship in relative freedom. We experience freedom of assembly, freedom of speech, freedom of political action, freedom of the press, and numerous other liberties. Consequently, we have a much greater obligation and responsibility to stand for social and economic justice for all men, women and children on this planet—especially for those who bear the great cost of being Christian where Christianity is not popular.

Our measure of economic justice must be that of the kingdom—that is, the bringing of good news to the poor, the binding up of hearts that are broken, and the proclamation of liberty to the captives. We must take a definite stand with those who are most vulnerable and in need of God's compassion.

As Christians, we have an awesome opportunity to use the freedoms we have been given to effect positive change, even eternal transformation, in the lives of others and in the corrupt systems and structures that presently influence our world. We should familiarize ourselves with the opportunities through education, printed literature and activities that we have been afforded to influence the course of events on our continent, as well as other continents of the world.

The church of Jesus Christ must stand with God against injustice, struggling side by side with the poor. Both corporately and individually, we must command the powerful global systems and structures and all demonic influences to fall prostrate before the rule and dominion of God. We must let economic justice roll like a river, and righteousness like a never-failing stream. We must be strong and courageous, fearlessly obeying the voice of the Spirit, which calls us to love and action.

Study 1

An Unjust World

Throughout the New Testament, we see Jesus moved with compassion for the multitudes who were politically and economically oppressed. He saw them as sheep without a shepherd, harassed, exploited and utterly helpless. He recognized that they were entrapped by corrupt systems and structures that were often demonically influenced. He knew that our world is intolerably unjust.

The existence of these evil influences should not be surprising to believers, because the Bible speaks plainly about the wages of sin, the fall of humankind, the need for reconciliation, and the powers and authorities in heavenly realms. With such negative influences, how could the world be anything but corrupt?

As twentieth-century believers, we tend to think of powers and authorities in terms of structures. Whether religious, political, moral, social or economic, all are powerful in their function, yet vulnerable to evil. If this is true, one can assume that the Israelites in their exodus from Egypt confronted the same kind of power structures that Peter and John confronted in the first century, that Martin Luther faced in the sixteenth century, and that you and I encounter in the twentieth century.

Remember that while the world order is blatantly unjust for the masses, a select few are living quite comfortably. This minority—the inhabitants of the industrialized North—is greatly contributing to the widening gulf that separates the nations of our world.

1. Who in our culture would you describe as poor?

Read Luke 6:17-26.
2. Jesus calls the poor blessed (v. 20). How can this be?

3. Why do you suppose he promises the poor the kingdom of God?

4. List three specific attributes that distinguish the first group, the poor (vv. 20-22), from the second, the rich (vv. 24-26).

5. Jesus, teaching his disciples, contrasts the rewards of the rich and the poor (vv. 20-26). What do you think was the primary objective of his teaching?

What does this mean within the context of contemporary society?

6. Are the poor you identified in our culture different from the poor in this passage?

7. Think of a poor individual or family in your community (or others you have heard about). Are they experiencing the kingdom of God in their lives? Why or why not?

Read Matthew 4:1-11.
8. It is essential that we remember that "our struggle is not against flesh and blood" (Eph 6:12), but against demonic powers. What specific temptation did Jesus face in terms of justice (v. 9)?

What would that temptation look like in modern terms?

Read 1 John 2:15-17.
9. Why are we told not to love the world (v. 15)?

10. Explain how the pull of the world could lead us to an unjust lifestyle.

11. *Response:* Scripture clearly teaches us that "the earth is the LORD's, and everything in it, the world, and all who live in it" (Ps 24:1). We have been called to be stewards of the Lord's earth. How does this affect the biblical call to justice?

What responsibility do you as a Christian have in this regard? Explain.

For Further Study: James 2:1-10; 5:1-6.

Study 2

Money and God's Servants

Christians of all denominations struggle with the uncomfortable words of Jesus about wealth and prosperity. For example, "A man's life does not consist in the abundance of his possessions" (Lk 12:15), and "the deceitfulness of wealth" chokes the word of God in our lives, "making it unfruitful" (Mt 13:22).

Money of itself is not evil, but "the love of money is a root of all kinds of evil" (1 Tim 6:10). Thus we must guard ourselves so that we do not allow the seduction and deceit of money to lord over our lives. Our economic lives (savings and investments, for example) must come under kingdom dominion just as every other area of our lives does.

Just as God's justice is a demonstration of his love for us, so our giving to the poor is a demonstration of our love and fidelity to him. Jesus calls some believers to "downward mobility." It is there that they truly experience the tension and conflict of being with the poor. All of us are called to invest our wealth in kingdom endeavors and to believe God for the return. He calls all of us to an inner freedom from the seduction of money and to sacrificial generosity and commitment of heart to the poor.

God has not called all people to be poor—but he has called us to be with the poor. He desires for us to follow his example and identify with the poor (Phil 2:5-8; 2 Cor 8:9), struggle with the poor (Phil 2:1-5; Rom 12:5), and provide for the poor (Prov 19:17; Mt 25:31-40). Read these passages.

1. Why do you suppose Christ's teachings about wealth (see the Scriptures above) make so many Christians uncomfortable?

How do they make you feel?

Read Matthew 19:16-30.
2. How did Jesus answer the rich young man's question about eternal life (vv. 17, 21)?

3. Why do you think Jesus answered in this way?

4. Why do you suppose it is harder for a rich person to enter the kingdom of God than for a camel to go through the eye of a needle (v. 24)?

5. Why were Jesus' disciples greatly astonished by his words about rich people and the kingdom of God (v. 25)?

6. Compare and contrast what the disciples may have believed about who would enter the kingdom of God with what contemporary Christians—as well as non-Christians—believe.

7. Reread verses 27-30. What have you sacrificed or forfeited to enter the kingdom of God?

What are you anticipating receiving in this life and the next?

8. What is meant by the statement in verse 30 "Many who are first will be last, and many who are last will be first"?

Read Luke 16:13.
9. According to this verse why is it impossible to serve two masters?

10. How does money become our master?

11. *Response:* What steps can you take to avoid serving the wrong master?

For Further Study: Matthew 6:19-24; Luke 12:33-34; 1 Timothy 6:17-19.

Study 3

Jubilee

The jubilee principle is one of the most radical teachings in all of Scripture. (At least it seems that way to twentieth-century people.) Every fifty years, not only did the land return to its original owner, but all debts were canceled and slaves were released.

Jesus, when speaking about the kingdom of God, used images and analogies reminiscent of the Sabbath and the year of jubilee. In his inaugural address (Lk 4:18-21), Jesus announced liberation of the captives and the oppressed. Further, Jesus' acts of compassion toward individuals as well as the masses demonstrated that he wanted people to be free from oppressive and exploitive structures.

The jubilee principle stands for release and for the demand that each human being has a right to return to what we all lost at the Fall. All people deserve freedom and sustenance for life. Captivity through debt or slavery is not God's best. The jubilee principle envisages the restoration of freedom and equality for all people regardless of their present socioeconomic status.

God himself has renounced the right to demand repayment of the debt we owe him. He has not used his power to crush us, but sent Christ to pay our debt in full, so that we might receive his forgiveness and be adopted into his family. How then can we—God's forgiven people—countenance an international order that oppresses the poor, pushing many of them to the brink of death in their efforts to repay the exorbitant interest on their debts?

1. The jubilee principle is one of liberation. From what has Christ liberated you?

Read Leviticus 25:8-43.

2. What did the jubilee provide for men and women every fiftieth year (vv. 10-22)?

3. What verse do you think best describes the spirit of the jubilee year? Why?

4. What do you suppose is the reason God instituted the jubilee year (v. 38, 42-43)?

5. The poor are specifically mentioned three times in this passage. Cite these Scriptures.

What does God say about how they are to be treated during the time of jubilee?

6. Contrast the way in which the poor are treated today with the way in which these poor Israelites were to be treated.

Read Matthew 18:21-35.
7. Think of a time that another person forgave you of a debt. How did it make you feel?

8. Describe an incident of unforgiveness that you have witnessed.

9. What message was Jesus communicating to Peter through this parable?

Why do you suppose this issue is so difficult for some Christians?

10. In view of our present global economic crisis, how could we possibly apply the principles of jubilee to our world?

11. The jubilee principle is more than the release of land, freeing of slaves and debt forgiveness. It represents God's restoration of every human's right to freedom and sustenance. What is standing in the way of human rights in the world today?

12. *Response:* Suggest at least three ways in which the principles of jubilee could be applied to the poor in your community.

For Further Study: Deuteronomy 15:1-18.

Study 4

The Global Community

Our planet is a global village. For the first time in history, technology and communications have linked us all together. There is more interaction between nations and peoples than at any time since the Tower of Babel. We have the potential to overcome great barriers as we act in community.

God's universal church, some 1.6 billion strong, is also interconnected. Although we come from different backgrounds, speak different languages, and hold diverse positions in the church and in our communities, we are corporately the body of Christ—the fullness of him who fills everything in every way. We can celebrate the unity of our diversity.

The earliest Christian church, founded in Jerusalem on the day of Pentecost, was characterized by profound fellowship. These believers voluntarily sold their possessions to provide for the needs of the community. "No one claimed that any of his possessions was his own" (Acts 4:32). They were free from the seduction of wealth and selfish assertions of property rights. As a result of their economic perspective, "there were no needy persons among them" (Acts 4:34).

Christ calls us to community, both locally and globally. We are to be salt and light in order to expose social ills and eliminate darkness. We must maintain our shine and saltiness in a world that fosters the widening gap between the "haves" and "have-nots."

1. Explain what is meant by the term *global community.*

What twentieth-century events and developments have contributed to this phenomenon?

Read Acts 4:32-37.
2. In this passage how does Luke describe the believers (vv. 32, 34-35)?

3. Why is Barnabas called *Son of Encouragement* (vv. 36-37)?

4. Some would say that Luke is advocating communal living because of his emphasis on sharing material wealth within the family of God.

What do you think he was advocating in this passage?

5. What was the significance of saying that "all the believers were one in heart and mind"?

6. Give three examples of how this passage can be applied in the theology and practice of the twentieth-century church.

Read Acts 5:1-11.
7. What was the sin of Ananias and Sapphira (v. 2)?

8. Who does Peter say that they have sinned against (vv. 3-4)?

9. Why did they die (v. 9)?

10. What do we learn from this passage about sharing with needy people in our community?

When are you tempted to imitate what Ananias and Sapphira did in your own giving?

11. *Response:* It would appear from the biblical account that New Testament Christians viewed themselves as so closely linked to each other that if one hurt, they all hurt. Their true understanding of community wouldn't let them ignore the poor—for that would be forsaking their very own flesh and blood. How does this profound sense of community affect your understanding of your church life?

What can you do about it? Be specific.

For Further Study: Matthew 26:6-13; Mark 14:3-9; John 12:1-8; Acts 4:34.

Study 5

God's Desire
for Justice

The Bible is filled with passages that relate to our economic life.
Both Old and New Testaments abound with references to money,
poverty, land, business, trade, production, livelihood, wealth and the
distribution of goods. Most passages speak about God's concern for
the poor and disenfranchised, while others highlight God's justice in
economics and the protection of the rights of all.

The Bible also tells of struggles between the rich and their powerful
institutions on one hand and the poor on the other. The latter were
often abandoned by everyone except God and a few prophets in the
Old Testament, and everyone except Jesus and the first-century
church in the New Testament. A remnant has always heard God's
voice and done what is just.

A theological statement on Christian Faith and Economic Justice
was approved in 1964 by the 196th General Assembly of the Pres-
byterian Church. It reads:

Whatever else the God of the Bible is, this One is a God of justice
(Isaiah 30:18). God loves justice (Isaiah 61:8), delights in justice
(Jeremiah 9:24), executes justice (Psalm 140:12), promises to es-
tablish justice (Isaiah 42:4), and demands justice (Deuteronomy

16:20). Whatever else honoring this God entails, it requires that we hunger and thirst after God's righteousness which includes God's justice (Matthew 5:6), that we seek God's kingdom and God's justice above all else (Matthew 6:33), and that we follow justice and only justice in our common life (Deuteronomy 16:20). The justice of God . . . is one of the Bible's greatest and most pervasive themes.

In the Bible God's justice is not something opposed to God's love but a manifestation of it. The two ideas are closely associated in such passages as these: "The Lord is just in all his ways, and loving in all his doings" (Psalm 145:17). God "executes justice for the fatherless and the widow, and loves the sojourner, giving him food and clothing" (Deuteronomy 10:18). Justice is God's love distributed. It is displayed especially in God's deliverance of those in need. "The Lord maintains the cause of the afflicted, and executes justice for the needy" (Psalm 140:12). It is God "who executes justice for the oppressed; who gives food for the hungry" (Psalm 146:5-7).

1. What, in your experience, has taught you that God loves justice and requires justice for all?

Read all the Scriptures listed above.
2. Based on the verses in the first paragraph of the statement above, define justice.

3. Describe what was happening in at least four of the passages above that led to God's implementing justice.

4. In what ways has God demonstrated his loving justice for you?

5. Obedience to God's will (loving God) and economic justice (or any other kind) are inseparable. List at least three outcomes of not following the biblical example of justice.

6. Describe at least three contemporary structures (institutions) that are economically oppressive, and explain why you consider them to be unjust.

What is their rationale for their actions?

7. List at least four biblical references we have studied so far in which God is portrayed as choosing a side.

8. "God always takes his stand unconditionally and passionately on the side of the poor. In fact, he is partial to them in every situation." Do you agree or disagree with this statement? Why or why not?

9. Identify at least three individuals or groups who have been denied justice today. What can be done to reverse this situation?

10. What generally happens in contemporary society when individuals commit themselves to a just cause, taking a firm stand and then acting on it?

11. Cite an example in which someone has advocated justice on behalf of the poor and oppressed. What was the result?

12. *Response:* When have you failed to stand with biblical justice to aid someone in need? How would you handle this situation differently?

Study 6

Christians Mobilize

Too often, good-willed, highly spirited Christians are immobilized by the size and complexity of social justice issues. Some of us question whether we would stand alone if we tried to take action against personal and structural injustice. Worse yet, some of us even question where God stands on issues of grave injustice.

In spite of our ever-changing human emotions, deep down we know through God's Word and Spirit that we have been called to take a stand for righteousness and justice. This call for action against injustice is both individual and corporate, and is not bound by geographic, political or socioeconomic limits.

As individuals confronted by the enormity of the task before us—multitudes unreached by the gospel, moral and spiritual apathy in the church, unbelievable poverty, violations of human rights, and economic exploitation—we are tempted to view the task as hopeless. What can one individual do? What possible good could be achieved by my contribution? What can my small efforts accomplish against principalities and powers?

And what about the corporate Christian community (local churches, campus fellowships, Bible study groups)? What could our church or Bible study group achieve? What areas of social justice could we pioneer in our communities? What differences could we make?

As Christians, we are called to take risks in order that we might be all that we can be for the kingdom. Our mandate, like that of the first-century church, is to begin with where we are and then to spread our influence to other cities, states and nations—even to the ends of the earth.

1. When have you seen an individual or small group of people make a difference in your community or in the world?

Read Matthew 25:31-46.
2. What differentiates the sheep from the goats (vv. 35-36, vv. 42-43)?

3. When is the decision made about who would be sheep or goats?

4. Why do you think Jesus focuses on things like hunger, thirst, hospitality and clothing?

What are the implications of this focus for ministry?

5. Who are the hungry, thirsty, strangers, naked and prisoners in your community?

How can you or your church directly minister to their needs?

Read James 2:14-26.
6. In verse 17 James says, "Faith by itself, if it is not accompanied by action, is dead." Why do you suppose that God requires us to demonstrate faith and works, not simply faith or works?

7. In verse 18 James writes, "Show me your faith without deeds, and

I will show you my faith by what I do." How are you showing your faith by what you do?

8. List three specific benefits outlined in verses 21-26 that result from faith and actions working together.

For final review, read Amos 2:6-7; 4:1-2; 5:11; 6:4-7; 8:4-6; 9:8.
9. Write your own definition of the Christian's call to the ministry of justice.

10. *Response:* Share your definition with others. Close by praying for a heart of justice.

For Further Study: Compare James with Romans 3:23-24 and Ephesians 2:8-9 and consider how these passages work together.

Suggestions for Leaders

Leading a Bible discussion can be an enjoyable and rewarding experience. But it can also be intimidating—especially if you've never done it before. If this is how you feel, you're in good company. When God asked Moses to lead the Israelites out of Egypt, he replied, "O Lord, please send someone else to do it!" (Ex 4:13). But God's response to all of his servants—including you—is essentially the same: "My grace is sufficient for you" (2 Cor 12:9).

There is another reason you should feel encouraged. Leading a Bible discussion is not difficult if you follow certain guidelines. You don't need to be an expert on the Bible or a trained teacher. The suggestions listed below should enable you to effectively and enjoyably fulfill your role as leader.

Preparing for the Study

1. Ask God to help you understand and apply the passage in your own life. Unless this happens, you will not be prepared to lead others. Pray too for the various members of the group. Ask God to open your hearts to the message of his Word and motivate you to action.

2. Read the introduction to the entire guide to get an overview of the subject at hand and the issues which will be explored. If you want to do more reading on the topic, check out the resource section at the end of the guide for appropriate books and magazines.

3. As you begin each study, read and reread the assigned Bible passages to familiarize yourself with them. Read the passages suggested for further study as well. This will give you a broader picture of how these issues are discussed throughout Scripture.

4. This study guide is based on the New International Version of the Bible. It will help you and the group if you use this translation as the basis for your study and discussion.

5. Carefully work through each question in the study. Spend time in meditation and reflection as you consider how to respond.

6. Write your thoughts and responses in the space provided in the study guide. This will help you to express your understanding of the passage clearly.

7. It might help you to have a Bible dictionary handy. Use it to look up any unfamiliar words, names or places. (For additional help on how to study a passage, see chapter five of *Leading Bible Discussions,* IVP.)

8. Take the response portion of each study seriously. Consider what this means for your life—what changes you might need to make in your lifestyle and/or actions you need to take in the world. Remember that the group will follow your lead in responding to the studies.

Leading the Study

1. Begin the study on time. Open with prayer, asking God to help the group to understand and apply the passage.

2. Be sure that everyone in your group has a study guide. Encourage the group to prepare beforehand for each discussion by reading the introduction to the guide and by working through the questions in the study.

3. At the beginning of your first time together, explain that these studies are meant to be discussions, not lectures. Encourage the members of the group to participate. However, do not put pressure on those who may be hesitant to speak during the first few sessions.

4. Have a group member read the introductory paragraph at the beginning of the discussion. This will orient the group to the topic of the study.

5. Have a group member read aloud the passage to be studied. (When there is more than one passage, the Scripture is divided up throughout the study so that you won't have to keep several passages in mind at the same time.)

6. As you ask the questions, keep in mind that they are designed to be used just as they are written. You may simply read them aloud. Or you may prefer to express them in your own words. There may be times when it is appropriate to deviate from the study guide. For example, a question may have already been answered. If so, move on to the next question. Or someone may raise an important question not covered in the guide. Take time to discuss it, but try to keep the group from going off on tangents.

7. Avoid answering your own questions. If necessary, repeat or rephrase them until they are clearly understood. An eager group quickly becomes passive and silent if they think the leader will do most of the talking.

8. Don't be afraid of silence. People may need time to think about the question before formulating their answers.

9. Don't be content with just one answer. Ask, "What do the rest of you think?" or "Anything else?" until several people have given answers to the question.

10. Acknowledge all contributions. Try to be affirming whenever possible. Never reject an answer. If it is clearly off-base, ask, "Which verse led you to that conclusion?" or again, "What do the rest of you think?"

11. Don't expect every answer to be addressed to you, even though this will probably happen at first. As group members become more at ease, they will begin to truly interact with each other. This is one sign of healthy discussion.

12. Don't be afraid of controversy. It can be very stimulating. If you don't resolve an issue completely, don't be frustrated. Move on and keep it in mind for later. A subsequent study may solve the problem.

13. Periodically summarize what the group has said about the passage. This helps to draw together the various ideas mentioned and gives continuity to the study. But don't preach.

14. Don't skip over the response question. Be willing to get things started by describing how you have been convicted by the study and what action you'd like to take. Consider doing a service project as a group in response to what you're learning from the studies. Alternately, hold one another accountable to get involved in some kind of active service.

15. Conclude your time together with conversational prayer. Ask for God's help in following through on the commitments you've made.

16. End on time.

Many more suggestions and helps are found in *The Small Group Leader's Handbook* and *Good Things Come in Small Groups* (both from IVP). Reading through one of these books would be worth your time.

Resources

Publications

Birch, Bruce, and Rasmussen, Larry. *The Predicament of the Prosperous.* Philadelphia: Westminster Press, 1978.

Costas, Orlando E. *Liberating News: A Theology of Contextual Evangelization.* Grand Rapids: Eerdmans, 1989.

Delamaide, Darrell. *Debt Shock: the Full Story of the World Credit Crisis.* Garden City, N.Y.: Doubleday, 1984.

George, Susan. *A Fate Worse Than Debt.* New York: Grove Press, 1988.

Lee, Robert. *Faith and the Prospect of Economic Collapse.* Atlanta: John Knox Press, 1981.

Lombardi, Richard W. *Debt Trap.* New York: Praeger, 1985.

"The Oxford Declaration on Christian Faith and Economics" (issued by the Oxford Conference on Christian Faith and Economics, January 1990). Available from Evangelicals for Social Action, 10 E. Lancaster Pike, Philadelphia, PA 19151; (215) 645-9390.

Perkins, John. *Let Justice Roll Down.* Ventura, Calif.: Regal Books, 1976.

Perkins, John. *With Justice for All.* Ventura, Calif.: Regal Books, 1982.

Rasmussen, Larry. *Economic Anxiety and Christian Faith.* Ventura, Calif.: Augsburg Press, 1981.

Sider, Ronald J. *Non-violence, the Invincible Weapon?* Dallas: Word, 1989.

Sider, Ronald J. *Rich Christians in an Age of Hunger: A Biblical Study.* 3rd ed. Dallas: Word, 1990.

Sider, Ronald J., ed. The Chicago Declaration. Carol Stream, Ill.: Creation House, 1974.

Wallis, Jim. *Agenda for Biblical People.* New ed. San Francisco: Harper & Row, 1984.

Film/Video

El Norte

Salvador